EYES ·OF· MANN

Photography and Text: Charles Guard
Drone Pilot: Glenn Whorrall
Editor: Miles Cowsill

PO Box 33 Ramsey Isle of Man IM99 4LP
Tel 01624 898446
email lilypubs@manx.net
web www.lilypublications.co.uk
© 2018 Lily Publications Ltd.

◀ **Castle Rushen,** Castletown's
greatest treasure.

RL360°

International House,
Cooil Road, Douglas
Isle of Man IM2 2SP

Tel: +44 (0) 1624 681 682
Fax +44 (0) 1624 677 336

email: csc@rl360.com

www.rl360.com

INTRODUCTION

In the last few years there has been an extraordinary coming together of various pieces of technology, all developed independently but which, when combined, have produced the phenomenon of drone photography.

The continuous search for miniaturisation and the constant improvement of the holding power of batteries have greatly contributed to this development, along with increasingly sophisticated lenses in miniaturised forms.

Add in lighter and stronger materials, GPS and more sophisticated electronics and all the pieces were in place to produce small, lightweight flying machines that could carry a camera, record large data files and be remotely controlled.

Drones come in varying sizes, and prices can vary widely too, from the highest quality professional models which come in at around £30,000, to the small, hobbyist ones, which can be picked up for a few hundred pounds. Just to be technical for a moment, the drone Glenn Whorrall and I have been using is the DJI Inspire 2, fitted with a Zenmuse X5S camera, using various Olympus lenses between 12mm and 25mm. It takes two of us to do the filming: Glenn flies the drone, using a remote controller and views progress on an iPad, I work the camera, moving it around as the subject requires also using a remote controller and monitoring what I film on an iPad.

Glenn and I spent the summer of 2018 praying for good weather, and, when we got it, dashing round the Island photographing and videoing a long list of locations.

I have been making films about the Island since the mid-1980s, and it's always been my guiding principle to make the Island look as good as possible. There was a time when I knew the seasons so intimately I could almost say which week a particular May tree would be in bloom because I knew there was a good shot of it against a certain backdrop.

However, the summer of 2018 proved to be a challenge. The first problem was the 'beast from the east', the surge of fiercely cold winter at the beginning of the year, sent over from Russia, with accompanying easterly gales. This had the effect of withering many plants such as the gorse. When it came to the early Spring, although the gorse flowered, the bushes themselves were a dull brown instead of the deep, vibrant green that they usually are.

However, worse was to follow. There was a prolonged period when very little rain fell. The whole of Britain was suffering from a magnificent, sun-drenched summer. We complain about the weather, no matter what it is doing. We long for sunny summers but when we get them they are too hot, or too dry, and it wasn't long before we were complaining that it was now too hot for too long. It did turn out to be the third warmest June in a series since 1910 and eventually a hosepipe ban came into force on the Island. The average temperatures were between 2 and 3 °C above average in most areas and rainfall was around 48% of average in most places, and in some areas of Britain a mere 10% of the average. It was this that made the difference for us photographers. Gradually the grass, the fields, the whole landscape started to turn brown. Looking over the northern plain towards the Pont of Ayre in July was like looking across a parched, southern Mediterranean landscape.

Some of the shots in this book reflect this unusual year. The chasms, for example, normally have a stunning contrast between the grey, crumbling slate and the lush, green grass. This is heightened in early

◀ The majestic shape of **North Barrule** dominates the landscape around Maughold.

◄ **The Northern Plain** is made up entirely of sand and gravel deposited here during the last Ice Age. Constant erosion over the past 10,000 years means that farmland is gradually falling into the sea. At their highest, at Shellag Point, the cliffs rise to over 200ft and are constantly being undermined by the action of waves and wind.

▲   Looking south over
Carraghan and Injebreck, the
southern hills are silhouetted by
the setting winter sun.

► Looking down onto **Loch Promenade** with the boarding houses facing the Sunken Gardens. A great change is due here as the scheme to resurface the promenade has started at last!

August when the late flowering gorse comes out and its yellow mixes with the vibrant purple of the heather. That didn't happen this year. Although some heather came into bloom, it was a shadow of its normal appearance and the mix of yellow and purple that is so striking at the chasms and also at the Point of Ayre, hardly happened at all.

Indeed, the extraordinary splash of colour provided by the heather on the Calf of Man and many of the Manx hills, was almost entirely missing this year. Nevertheless, as you'll see from the book, there was much else to capture.

When I made the video Isle of Man From the Air over fifteen years ago, I did all the filming from a helicopter and actually, compared to using a drone, it was much quicker and cheaper. Using a helicopter you can cover the entire Island in just over two hours, with one stop at Ronaldsway for refuelling. At around £1,800 an hour the whole process was done for less than £4,000.

However, using a drone is much more complicated. For a start, the cost of the drone and camera is much more than £4,000 and by the time you've added in spare batteries, iPads and so on, hiring a helicopter seems a bargain.

There's also the fact that the drone can only stay airborne for ten or fifteen minutes before you have to bring it in and change the batteries. Leaving it up any longer would mean that you were in danger of flying with less power than it would take to return to base. If you're out over the sea or above high cliffs, this is not recommended.

Yes, anyone can buy and fly a drone. But if you're using the resultant images for commercial purposes, you have to be insured and also have permission for aerial work from the Isle of Man Civil Aviation Administration. To get this permission the pilot has to pass a rigorous exam, with lots of technical paperwork and a practical exam as well. Of course, this is nonsensical. If you're not selling your footage you don't need any training at all; if you are, you do. This means there are lots of 'pilots' out there flying their drones for fun with no training or insurance and scant knowledge of the rules about launching away from roads and

people, and about the height and distance restrictions that govern commercial flyers. It's hard to understand what difference selling or not selling your photographs afterwards makes to the competence of the drone pilot, although I expect to see this change in the near future with rumours of new regulations on the table.

What is clear is that drone technology has crept up on the authorities so quickly that it has taken them by surprise, and the regulations and control of them is piecemeal. It must be rather like the advent of the motorcar. A free-for-all to begin with, but gradually, over the generations, licences are only issued to those passing a written and practical exam; no doubt, one day, this will be a requirement of all drone flying as well.

The other, major time-consuming factor of drone filming is that you need permission from the landowner to launch the drone. Of course, you can try it on spec and hope no one notices, but best practice is to get permission. I have therefore spent considerable time driving round the Island knocking on people's doors, or telephoning them, to seek permission to launch from their land. This includes farmers, friends, local commissioners, Manx National Heritage, the Ports and Harbours Authorities and many others besides. It was so much simpler in a helicopter, you just flew wherever you wanted and got on with it though, of course, the drone gives you an intimacy with a subject that a helicopter can never give as you can fly from ground level up to 400ft, whereas a helicopter is not allowed under 500ft.

One particular issue is flying the drone within a certain radius of the airport. Filming over Castletown or Langness, for example, requires special permission and co-ordination with Air Traffic Control at Ronaldsway. The best time for filming Castletown is a Saturday afternoon or a Sunday morning, this is when flight frequency is at its lowest and you are more likely to get half-an-hour or so clear, to sweep over the town. However, there was a particular issue with actually filming right next to the airport. When Glenn tried it (with permission from the Control Tower) he found that the drone's software came up with a great red

◄ **Douglas Marina** provides a safe haven for dozens of yachts and small boats. It was developed during the 1980s and has transformed Douglas Harbour. Previously, there was just mud when the tide went out but now, alongside new walkways and outdoor cafes, it is a colourful backdrop for those enjoying a morning coffee or lunch in the sun.

warning line around the airfield and it wouldn't fly. Apparently the drone company, DJI, lock every airport in the world in this way, stopping you flying over them. The only way the filming could be done was by Glenn contacting DJI in Shenzen, China, confirming their permission for Glenn to overfly Ronaldsway, and then for Glenn to receive a temporary 'unlocking' software modification via a download, to allow him to take the footage. I suppose it's reassuring that at least one manufacturer is taking the threat of drones hitting aircraft seriously. Their App doesn't include blocking filming of the TT though – this has to be done by the Manx authorities issuing a no-fly zone around the course during practices and races.

Is drone filming intrusive? Well, it can be, but then we accept the fact that all our houses are clearly visible on Google Earth and even more detail is available on Google Street View. We only had one problem whilst filming and that was from a gentleman who came rushing along to us asking what we were doing. He had bought his house in a remote location for privacy and didn't want us flying a drone over his property; besides, he told me, his wife often sunbathed nude in the back garden. I assured him we hadn't seen her so far and anyway, it wasn't his house we were interested in but the landscape roundabout. He left. Within a few minutes he was back again saying that he was going to move his van and we could film his house but definitely not his back garden. It was only when I got the footage back to the studio and looked at it on a big screen I could see why he was so concerned. He was in the process of building the most appalling extension on the back of his house, one which, (how can I put it?) I doubt the Planning Committee would ever agree to. Of course, we haven't used any of that footage and there was no sign of his wife

It's been a long process, and taken may trips out into the Manx countryside (but what better way to spend a summer?) and around the towns and villages of the Island, and it's been something of a revelation. As I remark in the captions, the dazzling terraces of Douglas can only really be appreciated from the air, and the sea of bungalows and housing estates around many of the other towns and villages also, is only really visible from above.

I would like to thank all of those people and organisations that have allowed us access to film from their land, and a very big thank-you to Glenn for his patience and for his willingness to become involved in such a long and complicated project, and for seeing it through to the end.

In the early days of filming I had found it rather difficult to see the images on the iPad when out in the glaring sunshine, and so I tried various options, including hunching myself under a cape to try and create a mini dark room. Glenn was far too polite to say how embarassing this must have been for him to be seen alongside, but the discrete emailing of a photograph made the point, and I stopped.

Of course, as well as hundreds of photographs, we also took hours of stunning video footage. All of this will be available over the coming months in a series of short videos I will be producing online. I'll be dealing with all sorts of subjects – coastal erosion, the castles and forts, the Tholtans, the history of mining, the towns and villages &c., using our unique drone footage. It will be free to watch or download from my website: **www.charlesguard.com** and will be in a series called 'Charles Guard's Isle of Man From the Air – with Drones'.

Charles Guard
October 2018

▶ **The Tower of Refuge** clings to Conister Rocks in Douglas Bay like a limpet, its rounded towers repelling the seas that have battered it since it was constructed in 1832.

EYES OF MANN

DOUGLAS & THE EAST

▲ **Douglas Harbour** stands ready to welcome the Isle of Man Steam Packet's fast craft *Manannan*. The Masters of these craft are highly skilled at carrying out three-point turns in a small space on arrival, and gently backing the vessel onto its linkspan berth.

▶ **Douglas Marina** is lit by the early morning sun long before the onset of commuter traffic that will pour in from the south as the start of the working day approaches.

◀ It was when arriving in Douglas Bay in 1833 that the future Poet Laureate, William Wordsworth, wrote a poem in tribute to Manx resident Sir William Hillary whose heroic efforts to save lives at sea eventually led to the founding of the Royal National Lifeboat Institute.

One of the most daring rescues had involved Sir William spending the night on the treacherous Conister rocks in a fierce storm, having safely taken the 20 crew members off the Royal Mail Packet Steamer *St George* which had foundered.

He later raised the money to build a small castle on the rocks, which was provisioned with water, kindling and basic supplies, so that anyone wrecked there in the future could wait out the storm in relative safety.

When he saw the castle and learnt of its purpose, Wordsworth wrote the poem *On Entering Douglas Bay* in which he described the castle as '**A Tower of Refuge**', and that's how it has been known ever since.

▶   Overlooking Douglas Harbour is the long, white frontage of Fort Anne. The present building is an office block but it stands on the site of a Gothic-style residence, built in the late 18th century, and once the home of Sir William Hillary. It was from here that he surveyed the harbour and was ready to venture out into all weathers to help sailors in distress.

In fact, he drew up bold and imaginative plans to extend the harbour and make it one of the finest shelters on the Irish Sea, but these never came to pass.
It was the increase in traffic in Victorian times that brought about the extension of the piers for deep-water berthing, the building of the breakwater (which was further extended in the early 1980s) and which led to the passenger facilities that we have today.

◄ The land around Douglas Harbour shows signs of its industrial past. Two huge quarries, believed to be amongst the earliest on the Island, are where a good deal of the building stone for early Douglas would have come from. They are now the locations for various industrial estates which have replaced the earlier gas works that provided street lighting and energy for the town in Victorian times.

In the foreground at least four major sites still await development, and are currently used as much-needed car parking space.

As long ago as the 1980s announcements were being made of grand new schemes for a hotel with public swimming facilities on the site which was once the Lord Street bus station.

We are still looking forward to these exciting developments.
Across the harbour bridge, with its blue tilting mechanism perched on two towers, is the tall Bridge Control Building which was constructed in 1895. It houses the amazing accumulator mechanism which swung the old harbour bridge back and forth as ships came and went from the inner harbour.

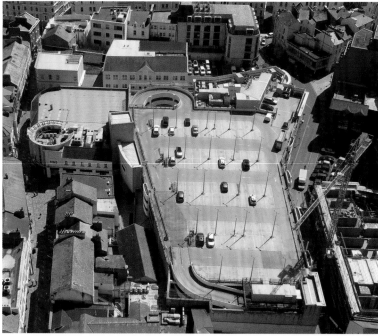

◀ One thing a drone allows you to do is look directly down on the streets and buildings of a town - a most unusual perspective.

On the *top left* we are looking down on the former Royal Bank of Scotland building (now renamed **Villiers House**) which few people know has a roof garden. The dry summer of 2018 meant the grass wasn't watered and it quickly turned brown.

On the *bottom left* is a view of **Victoria Street** at its intersection with Duke Street.

The *top right* photograph is higher up **Victoria Street** where it is joined by Thomas Street.

Finally, the *bottom right* photograph is looking down on the **Marks and Spencer** car park with the construction, on the right, of a new 85 bedroom Premier Inn hotel, hidden away in a back lane.

▶ A striking view of the **Sea Terminal** in Douglas, which clearly shows its architect's reference to the Three Legs of Man. It was opened in 1965.

◄ **Prospect Hill** is now one of the main routes from lower to upper Douglas. Athol Street (which joins the hill at the bottom left of the photograph) was first laid out in 1810 and one of the first buildings to appear was named Prospect Hill, presumably because it had a fine view over Douglas Bay. The name was later adopted for the nearby road itself.

The Isle of Man Bank head offices, Victory House, St Mary's Catholic Church and government offices all front onto Prospect Hill and the jumble of architectural styles is clearly visible from the air.

◄ **Mount Havelock** was once the site of a row of tall Victorian houses, all of which had a garden on the opposite side of the road but which have now become a car park. The grey building in the middle is Murray House, a 1980s office development which is now owned by the government and houses, amongst other things, the planning committee.

It is good to see that it has been refurbished in recent years and the ludicrous, full-height columns that once defaced its front have been removed (and hopefully buried). This view shows the consistency of earlier developments. The terraces, and even the individual houses of Finch Road (at the bottom of the photograph) have a certain unity about them. It's just the modern additions, including the courthouse to the upper left, that seem to struggle to have any resonance with their earlier neighbours.

▶ In the centre of this photograph of **lower Douglas** is Chester Street car park. This was built after the warren of Victorian streets, which included Chester Street, was demolished in the late 1960s.

The car park comes right alongside St Thomas' School (now closed) and St Thomas' church, which has stood there since 1847.

Castle Street and Strand Street thread their way behind the buildings that form the Douglas sea front. This aerial view shows something that is not so easy to appreciate from the ground - the amount of land that was reclaimed when Loch Promenade was built in the 1870s.

Strand Street was once right on the seashore, and all the land between it and the present sea wall has been reclaimed to make Douglas' magnificent promenade one of the finest in the British Isles.

▲ The splendid façades of the **Sefton Hotel** and the Gaiety Theatre provide some of the most striking architecture on the Douglas seafront. The hotel was opened in 1892 and designed by William John Rennison, an architect who had moved to the Island from Stockport. The small archways at the base of the two turreted sections were originally an entrance and exit for carriages that could drive around the back of the hotel to deliver guests and their luggage under cover.

The **Gaiety Theatre**, with its long barrelled roof, has one of the finest Victorian interiors of any theatre in Britain and was designed by Frank Matcham. It opened in 1900.

◄ One of the terraces of **Loch Promenade**, which were built in the mid-1870s after a bold scheme to reclaim a huge area of land from the sea. This terrace, and the adjacent ones, provide a magnificent, sweeping façade which is not rivalled in any other British seaside resort. Their uniformity, coupled with subtle variations in the superb decorative detail, make them one of the treasures of Manx architecture.

▲ **The Villa Marina** (*above and right*) is the Island's premier entertainment centre with catering facilities, function rooms, a cinema, children's area and, at its centre, a fine concert hall, which can seat up to 1,500 people.

◄ The Marine Gardens of **Loch Promenade** were opened in 1935 when a second promenade widening scheme was completed. Although their construction caused much annoyance to the Loch Promenade boarding houses, producing noise and dirt, the inconvenience was well worth it. Popularly known as the Sunken Gardens, during the summer they are full of interesting planting looked after by the Parks Department of Douglas Borough Council.

◄ **Central Promenade** in Douglas was the last section of the promenade to be officially opened, in 1896, but it actually contains some of the earliest buildings, including the Esplanade, built in the mid-1840s with a private walled garden in front, now with cars parked on the grass.

At the bottom of the photograph is the large development based around the original Crescent Cinema, the façade of which has been retained at one end of a series of apartments.

Directly behind is a terrace of houses along Castle Mona Avenue, the route of which was once the official driveway to the Duke of Atholl's private residence, the Castle Mona.

▶ The promenade walkway has some very distinctive patterning on its surface (*right*) made up of pink rectangles and smaller green squares set into the surrounding surface. Is it too much to hope that this will be retained in any future make-over?

Further along the promenade (*bottom right*) and opposite the Castle Mona, are blocks of boarding houses which stand on what was once the formal lawns of the Castle. The left-hand block is now apartments, replacing earlier boarding houses, and the red brick building at the centre bottom of the photograph, the Imperial, has since been demolished for redevelopment.

◀ The future of the **Castle Mona** has been of great concern in recent years as it was left standing unoccupied and has gradually deteriorated.

It was originally built in 1804 by the 4th Duke of Atholl, no doubt using some of the money the family had received from the British Government as compensation for being stripped of many of their rights and privileges as Lords of Man.

Not long afterwards the Atholls left the Island for good and the building was converted into a hotel. In the 1960s the right-hand wing was built to create more bedrooms, but the extension did little to enhance the property architecturally. The hotel closed in 2006 and, although its sale has been announced several times, it is only recently that this seems to have actually happened.

We await future developments with interest.

◄ A splendid view of some of the terraces halfway up **Broadway**. In the centre, with gardens down to the main road, is Stanley Terrace, built in 1836 and one of the earliest in the area. Beyond is Drury Terrace behind which is one of Douglas' fine town squares, Hutchinson Square. Barbed wire surrounded the houses that form the square when it became an internment camp during World War II, and the camp included Drury Terrace as well.

At the left of the photograph is the former Falcon Brewery (with scaffolding on its end) which was started by a Dr William Okell in the 1870s and is now apartments. The tree-covered top of Falcon Glen can be seen in front of it across the road.

▶ A view of the **Manx Museum**, headquarters of Manx National Heritage.
The large, square extension housing a lecture theatre and gallery is clearly visible, and to its left is the earlier part of the building which was originally built in 1888 as the first Noble's Hospital, with funds gifted to the town by Henry Bloom Noble and his wife, Rebecca.

It became the Manx Museum in 1922 and since then has been considerably extended. To the left is the 'stack', a tall building which houses the precious archives that Manx National Heritage curate for the nation. Running to the right are the backs of Mona Terrace which faces onto Chester Street car park.

▶ Douglas is blessed with some fine town squares and this one (*opposite page*) is **Derby Square**. Originally set out in the mid-1830s, the owner marked out 81 building plots with a further 16 plots on the north side to be called Derby Terrace. A strict covenant was levied on any developer, which detailed a uniform design and the preservation of the central, open area for residents. This is now maintained by Douglas Borough Council.

▶   Whereas many other towns on the Island sport acres of bungalows, the striking feature of Douglas is a wealth of terraces, only really appreciated from above. Remarkably, the integrity of most of these has been maintained (except, of course, for the inevitable introduction of uPVC window frames), and although there is no formal arrangement, the colours chosen by residents for external decoration presens a pleasing harmony.

In the centre foreground is a large, open space that once housed Park Road School, which was opened in 1894 and closed in 2012 and subsequently demolished. At the other end of the site is the Bowling Green Hotel, built in 1873 with twelve bedrooms, a croquet lawn and a large bowling green to its rear. The large red brick complex in the centre left of the photograph is the Waverley Court sheltered housing complex, operated by Douglas Borough Council. It stands on the site of the former Waverley Road car shed and engine house associated with the Upper Douglas Cable Tramway which ran between 1896 and 1929.

Most of the houses in this photograph would have been boarding houses at one time, as the Island welcomed more than 650,000 tourists a year in Edwardian times.

◄ A feature of Douglas town squares is their generous planting of trees, and this square (more of a triangle, really) is **Queen's Gardens**, formed by two facing terraces of Queen's Terrace and Queen's Avenue and Alexander Drive, which forms its third side where the popular Woodbourne Hotel stands.

Although building started in this area in 1883 it was a petition in 1887 that asked for the names of the roads to be changed to mark Queen Victoria's Golden Jubilee. Originally, like many other squares in the town, the surrounding residents were required to pay an annual sum (in this case, 25/-) to local trustees to pay for the upkeep of the gardens. This was abolished in 1949 when an Act of Tynwald transferred the responsibility for their upkeep to Douglas Borough Council.

▶ At the centre of the picture (*right*) is Freemason's Hall on **Woodbourne Road**, a large extension (completed in 1925) which dwarfs the small, but beautifully formed, Georgian house that it is attached to. Originally called Woodbourne House, it was once the home of the distinguished Manx scholar and Speaker of the House of Keys, A W Moore. Beyond the house can be seen the parched grass of Hillary Park.

Amongst the maze of terraces on either side of **Buck's Road** (*below right*) two buildings stand out: the striking roofs and spire of Trinity Methodist Church at Rosemount with its spacious halls behind, and beyond it to the right, the Kensington Road Youth Arts Centre, which was, at one time, the Douglas School of Art where Archibald Knox studied and later taught.

▶ **Brighton Terrace** (*opposite page*) faces on to an area of land in front of Eastfield which, in the 1850s, was destined for superior residences that never materialised, and covenants on the square have meant that it has remained as private, undeveloped land.

◄ **St Catherine's Drive** runs along the right-hand side of the photograph and across the bottom, enclosing an area of land given over to allotments, run by the Douglas Allotments Association, with a variety of sheds and greenhouses. To the extreme right is part of Ballakermeen School's playing fields. The whole area was developed in the 1930s on what was Ballakermeen farmland.

To the left is what remains of the old Noble's Hospital where some medical facilities are still housed and beyond that, the houses of Hillside Avenue.

▼ **Ballakermeen School** and playing fields are now surrounded by a sea of semi-detached houses. Completed in the late 1930s, the school was used during the war years by the Royal Navy to give sea cadets an education comparable to that of a secondary school. Called HMS *St George*, the cadets received a concentrated fifteen-month training course delivered by a staff of over 300.

Things are a bit different today. Ballakermeen High School is now a fully comprehensive secondary school serving Douglas. There are over 1,500 students aged 11 – 18 and it is the Island's largest secondary school.

▶ **Pulrose Power Station** was opened by HRH Prince Philip in 2003. He had opened a new power station on this site on his previous visit in 1989. The present one is gas-fired, using gas that has been brought across the Island from Glen Mooar where an undersea pipeline comes ashore. The station can produce nearly 135 megawatts of electricity and some of this can be exported to the UK when demand requires it.

In the foreground are the fans of the air-cooled heat exchanger which have replaced the huge cooling towers that once stood on this site.

◀ **Royal Avenue West** in **Onchan** looks over Port Jack Glen. The east and west terraces of the avenue were built between 1898 and 1906, the latter being constructed as boarding houses by Alexander Gill, one of the main developers of Douglas Promenade.

For a brief period in World War II parts of both terraces were commandeered by the British government for use as internment camps and they housed Germans, Austrians and later, Italians. The stream that runs through Port Jack Glen was, at one time, the tail race of the mill which stood at the bottom of Royal Avenue when all the area was meadow and part of Howstrake farm.

The glen itself was taken over by Onchan Commissioners in 1959 and developed by them and landscaped with paths and bridges and two ponds.

Towards the top right of the photograph you can see St Anthony's Catholic Church, built in the 1980s with monies given by Albert Gubay. He claimed he had a pact with God that if he became a millionaire he would give half of his estate to the Catholic Church on his death. He did indeed become a millionaire and left a substantial amount to the church, so it seems to have worked out well for both parties. The only question that remains is, who was Jack?

◄ This view of lower **Onchan** shows the popular Onchan Park, built on land bought by Onchan Village Commissioners after World War II who built a stadium and the first-ever banked cycle track on the Island.

There's now a grandstand, a cafe and other sports facilities as well as a boating lake with motor boats.

▶ In the centre of **Onchan** is St Peter's Church. Built in 1833 it replaced an earlier one, parts of which dated back to the 12th century. Apparently, it was the first church on the Island to be lit by electricity which was supplied by the Isle of Man Tramways and Power Company (or the Manx Electric Railway, as we call it today), and when the lights dimmed during Sunday evensong the congregation knew that a tram was pulling out of Derby Castle.

Onchan has grown enormously in recent years. At one time it was a small village north of Douglas, and in the 1850s it had just 51 houses, but during the late Victorian and Edwardian period it saw the extensive development of terraces of houses to accommodate the overflow of visitors from Douglas. Since then hundreds of houses have been built and nowadays the population is over 9,000 making Onchan the second largest population centre on the Island after Douglas.

▶ **St Ninian's Lower School** (*opposite page*) was opened in 2012 and caters for years seven to nine before they move on to St Ninian's Upper School at the top of Broadway.

◄ The apartments of **Majestic View** on the outskirts of Onchan stand on the site once occupied by the Majestic Hotel, which itself contained some earlier houses designed by Baillie Scott, one of the Arts and Crafts movement's most important architects.

Sadly, although making it onto the Island's register of protected buildings, they were removed from the list and then demolished along with the rest of the hotel. The headland beyond has now been developed with some large and expensive private dwellings, but none of this would have been possible if hadn't been for the Manx Electric Railway.

The tracks run along the road which was constructed in 1893 as part of the scheme to run the railway from Douglas to Laxey. This opened up the whole area for development. Originally the road was called Marine Drive, but this was changed in 1902 to King Edward Road after the surprise visit to the Island of King Edward VII and Queen Alexandra, who took the tram along here back to Ramsey to join the Royal yacht berthed at Queen's Pier.

◄ Looking across **Onchan** from its highest point you can see just how much it has pushed out into the countryside.

This, more than anything else, tells you how the economy of the Island has grown in recent decades. Generally, planning policy has required new developments to be the continuation of existing estates, and this has helped to keep the growing urbanisation confined to the edges of the towns and villages.

This policy has produced a happy knock-on effect for some landowners. On the edges of places like Douglas, the re-zoning of agricultural land as building land has meant that fields whose value was purely seen in terms of agriculture, were suddenly worth a small, and in some cases a very large, fortune.

Nearly all the land in this photograph was once farmed, and already the pressure is on to zone more land for more houses.

▶ The promenade at **Laxey** has become increasingly popular in recent years. Catering outlets supplying ice cream, soup, homemade cakes and other delights, have made the prom, with its sandy beach and nearby walks, a regular meeting place for many people.

The magnificent backdrop of Snaefell and the surrounding hills creates the perfect setting for the village of Laxey and its tidal harbour.

Many of the houses and cottages from the 19th century still stand, though it's hard to imagine the intense industrial activity that once took place around the harbour when the Great Laxey Mine was still active at that time.

◀ 2018 saw the 125th anniversary of the Manx Electric Railway, now the world's oldest surviving electric tramway running on its original tracks.

Laxey Station (*left*) is something of an interchange; trams come in from Douglas and Ramsey and passengers can change here to ride on another electric railway, the Snaefell Mountain Railway.

The striking viaduct that brings the trams across the Glen Roy river was built in just four months in 1898 by a local contractor, Mark Carine.

▼ **The Snaefell Mountain Railway** car shed is in the middle of the photograph (*below*) and the mountain railway tracks come down and run parallel with the coastal railway as they cross the road into Laxey Station.

◀ Car 1 and trailer 51 are about to depart from **Laxey Station** for Douglas (*opposite page*) and customers are queueing nearby to board a Snaefell Mountain Railway car. The fine weather at least guarantees spectacular views from Snaefell summit but even so, passenger numbers on all the railways have risen encouragingly in recent years as money has been invested in the systems' infrastructures and in marketing the Island's unique transport heritage around the world.

◄ Looking vertically down onto the **washing floors** in Laxey reveals some of the remains of an industry which was once the economic driver of the Isle of Man - mining. At the extreme bottom right is a glimpse of the Manx Electric Railway track but next to it are the smaller tracks of the Laxey Mines Railway, now restored, which once brought lead ore from deep underground.

The ore was tipped down the nearby chutes and sorted ready for crushing. In the centre of the picture is a small circle where there once stood a tall, brick chimney and beyond is the Lady Evelyn, a waterwheel turning on the exact site that an earlier wheel used in Victorian times. The area is now landscaped and known as the Valley Gardens.

◄ The **Cooil Roy** sheltered housing complex (*left*) faces the river and behind, running up to the Manx Electric Railway track, are the remains of huge piles of spoil - crushed stones that were extracted from the nearby mines in the 19th century.

► The sloping land of **South Cape** (*right*) provides some splendid vantage points for the houses that are accessed, in some cases, by narrow, winding roads that criss-cross the headland.

◀ How things have changed on **Laxey Promenade**. The car park in front of the old warehouse was once a walled compound in which crushed ore was stored prior to it being loaded into boats for export to the UK.

Mining was the all-absorbing occupation of Laxey through the 19th century, and thousands of tons of high-grade zinc ore were exported during those years. The quayside in the photograph was once known as Rowe's Dock, and next to it, Captain Rowe's warehouse: Richard Rowe being the captain of the Laxey mines between 1845 and 1872.

Many of the surrounding buildings actually survive from that period, and apart from the new sea wall and the change of use of some of the areas, this part of Old Laxey still retains much of its Victorian layout.

◀ The world's greatest waterwheel, the **Lady Isabella**, hardly needs any introduction. Built in 1854 by a Laxey-born engineer, Robert Casement, its massive 72 ft diameter was used to pump water from the nearby mine shafts that went down some 1,500 feet into the ground below.

The pumps are actually a good distance up the valley, and the energy of the turning wheel is conveyed to the head of the pump-shaft by a rod which is 630ft long. This rod is attached to a crank on the side of the wheel and is supported by a series of beautiful, stone-built arches.

The water to turn the wheel comes up the inside of the tower at its back. The water is gravity-fed from a small cistern further up the valley which is higher than the top of the tower and therefore requires no pump. Altogether, the wheel is elegant, practical, and a masterpiece of Victorian engineering.

RAMSEY &
THE NORTH

▲   Clagh Ouyr and North Barrule in the distance (*above*) have a light dusting of snow, but on a fine day the view from here is breathtaking. The view from Barrule's summit sweeps from the Point of Ayre and across Maughold Head to the wind farms of Lancashire beyond.

▶   Parts of **Maughold Church** (*opposite*) may date back to the 1100s and it is built on the site of a much earlier monastic settlement which was certainly occupied in the 6th century. Remains of early keeills, or small chapels, can be seen in the enclosure and there is also a cross house in which stand some 50 carved stone crosses, many of them more than a thousand years old. It is the finest collection on the Island

◄ **Maughold Head lighthouse** perches precariously above towering cliffs, and the light is attached to the keepers' house by a steep stairway.

It was completed in 1914 and built by the Stevenson family for the Northern Lighthouse Board. It is now automated, like all other lighthouses around Britain, and the house is privately owned.

Below the lighthouse are two beaches, and on the left-hand one can be seen the cave-like entrance to the Maughold Head mine. Quite how the miners got down there to go to work is something of a mystery, but the bands of quartz in the nearby rock are probably what attracted them to prospect there in the first place.

▼ On a beach just south of **Maughold Head** are the skeletal remains of a vessel. Apparently there had been an attempt to scupper this vessel out at sea in the 1940s by the then Harbour Board. It was something of a botched job, and before long it reappeared in this cove where it has been gently rotting ever since.

◄ The view of **South Ramsey** shows what happens when developers persuade a planning committee that the latest concrete structures and high-rise buildings are appropriate, regardless of their context.

In the late 1960s and early 70s much of old South Ramsey was swept away and new apartment blocks were built, being some of the first on the Island.

▲ Slightly further south the houses are on a more modest scale, though it seems that there is always room for apartments.

In the middle left of the photograph is what remains of the former Beach Hotel, now rebuilt and extended as The Fountains apartment block.
In the distance, where the beach ends, can be seen what looks like a landslip. It is being held in place by a line of boulders which are supporting the earth above and thereby stopping the tramlines from slipping down towards the beach.

◄ A view over **Ramsey Harbour** with the shipyard in the foreground. It was here that the world's first tanker was built, as well as the *Star of India,* which is now a floating museum in San Diego.

The government-owned shipyard has recently been taken over by Ramsey Shipping Services who are hoping to develop the site as an important ship repair service for Manx and non-Manx vessels.

The terraces of houses, which stand near the site of the old gasworks and salt works, have recently been joined by some modern apartments. These could have been looking out over a marina, at least, that was the plan. Nearly two decades ago there was an ambitious multi-million-pound scheme to develop this site with a marina, apartments and other facilities. However, there was a sustained campaign by a group calling itself Ramsey Against Insensitive Development (what a pity they weren't around in the early 70s), and the plans were dropped.

The Minister for Infrastructure recently confirmed, in the House of Keys, that his department was not progressing a marina plan at the moment, even though a public consultation in 2009 was strongly in favour of one.

▼   The south side of **Ramsey Harbour** is where the fishing boats tie up and the quayside buildings still retain much of their Victorian charm.

▶   The swing bridge in **Ramsey Harbour** was opened in 1892 after long delays due to technical difficulties and disputes. It paved the way for the development of the north Ramsey promenade.
Originally it was swung by two men winding handles connected to cogs and wheels. It was refurbished in 2013 and is now motorised.

◀ A splendid view of **South Ramsey** with the twins arms of the harbour piers offering a safe haven to vessels coming in from the Irish Sea.

But there's another pier as well, the Queen's Pier. Most people will know that it has been closed for years (since 1991) and is currently the subject of a restoration project, run by the Queen's Pier Restoration Trust, which seeks to bring it back to its former glory.

Originally opened in 1886, there was a time when more than 36,000 passengers a year would use it. By the 1970s though, with the decline in tourism, the pier was closed to steamers but was still used by pedestrians and anglers.

A survey done in 1999 showed that it was in much better condition than many other British piers, due in part to the advanced techniques used by its designer, Sir John Coode. Its woodwork might be rotting, but the supporting legs are as true and stable as the day they were built. The main body of the pier was 2,160 ft long, but with the addition of timbered fendering, it can claim to have been 2,248 ft long.

A bizarre and completely useless comparison has been pointed out to the author - if you stood the up pier on its end, it would be higher than Snaefell.

◄ The top two photographs show the work needed to restore **Ramsey Pier**. Some new timbering has been laid at the landward end, but there's still a long way to go.

► Ramsey really does 'shine by the sea' as the old song says and it is in a spectacular location at the foot of the northern hills. One of its prime attractions is the **Mooragh Park** (*right*) which was laid out in 1887, with the boating lake said to represent the shape of the Isle of Man.

◄ Once the swing bridge was in operation, the development of Ramsey's **North Promenade** (*far left*) could proceed. Plots were sold and boarding houses were built and Ramsey at last was able to cash in on the tourism bonanza in a big way. Ramsey's third swimming pool (*left*) replaces the 1902 open-air pool and a more recent pool south of the harbour.

► Waterloo Road coming in from the bottom centre of the photograph is one of the main routes into the town, especially when the Mountain Road is closed and traffic from Douglas has to use the coast road.

▼ **Milntown House**, on the outskirts of Ramsey, is the ancestral home of the Christian family, and for many generations the heads of the family were appointed as Deemsters. It was Deemster John Christian who added the extravagant Gothic façade in the 1830s, thereby transforming a rather simple Georgian house, which dated from the 1750s, into the present masterpiece. The Christians have long-since departed, and nowadays the entire estate is open to the public throughout the year.

▶ Just outside Sulby is an extraordinary natural feature known as **Cronk Sumark**, or Primrose Hill. Its steep sides rise up abruptly from the surrounding plain and it has, on its summit, the remains of an Iron Age or Early Christian hill fort, and the outline of ancient ramparts can just be discerned on this side of the hill. Though arduous, it is well worth the climb to the top from where the whole of the northern plain can be seen in one sweeping vista.

◄   The whole of the **Northern Plain** is a gift from the Ice Age. Before that period the Isle of Man's northern coastline was at the bottom of the northern hills. As the ice retreated it left behind a huge area of sand and gravel which has been gradually eroding ever since.

Nowadays, the exposed sand cliffs provide a dramatic sight and as the sea continues to eat away at their base, clumps of turf, fencing and sometimes even houses, fall onto the beach below.

► The **Point of Ayre Lighthouse** was first lit in 1818 after a long battle to get the importance of marking the treacherous Manx coast with lights recognised. Merchants from around the Irish Sea were constantly complaining, during the 18th century, that hazards such as the Chicken's Rock off the south of the Island were a permanent danger to their trade.

Eventually, the Duke of Atholl was persuaded to lease some land, and the Northern Lighthouse Board engaged their Chief Engineer, Robert Stevenson, to draw up plans to light the northern and the southern extremities of the Isle of Man.

There were many challenges, not least the shifting shoreline at the Point of Ayre. Since the light was first built, the Point has moved slowly round towards the south-east, due to the continuing accumulation of pebbles. This meant that eventually the lighthouse was further inland than originally intended, so a secondary light was added to the seaward side of the main tower in 1899, and, as the shingle continued to move, The Winkie, as it was nicknamed, was moved a further 250ft seawards where it now stands (*opposite page*).

Between the Winkie and the main light you can see the white tower supporting the twin horns of the old foghorn, last heard in 2005.

◄   The most northerly
settlement on the Island is the small
village of **Bride**, dominated by the
spire of its parish church.
The church dates from 1872, but it
houses a number of important early
stone crosses, one of which dates to
the late 10th century.

Things are a lot more peaceful in
Bride than they were 20 years ago
when every day, every refuse truck
on the Island would drive through
the village, thundering across the
roundabout, on its way to Wright's
Pit East at the Point of Ayre.
Tynwald had prevaricated so long
about building the incinerator,
which was behind schedule anyway,
and every other landfill site on the
Island was full, that digging a pit in
the sand at the Point to bury the
Island's rubbish was the only option
left.

Sadly, it was too near the sea and the
eroding cliffs are now getting
dangerously close to its edge. To
avoid an environmental disaster,
some say the only thing to do is to
dig the landfill out and cart it all
back down south again and burn it
in the incinerator.
Bride - enjoy the peace while it
lasts.

▶   Wherever there was an Anglican church, you would find a Methodist one nearby, if not two. **Bride** is no exception.

Just down from the Parish Church is the Lamb Hill road and there is Bride Methodist Church, built in 1877, replacing one that had been built in 1801, just twenty years after Methodism's founder, John Wesley, visited the Island.

▶   The parish church of Kirk Andreas (*opposite*) was opened in 1802, replacing a much earlier building. Its fine bell tower was added in 1869 and at one time was 120ft high. However, during the Second World War a large section of it was removed to lower its height on the orders of the War Ministry, as it was presenting a hazard to aircraft landing at nearby Andreas Airfield, operated by the RAF.

The intention had been to rebuild it after the war, but although the numbered stones were kept for a while, they now seem to have disappeared. On display inside the church are some exceptionally fine Viking carved stone crosses.

◄   Most of the villages on the Island are a mixture of an old, central part, surrounded by an ever-increasing belt of modern housing. This is the case in **Andreas Village** where numerous estates have spread out into the surrounding countryside.

Andreas sits in the middle of the northern plain, and this made it an ideal site for a World War II airfield for training pilots and navigators, and for servicing aircraft involved in the defence of Britain.

Those war years are not forgotten as several of the buildings around the village date from that period, most notably the village hall which is a classic, brick-built WWII building.

◄ The strange pattern in the field behind these houses in **Sulby** is actually an important safeguard for the village. In the late 1990s the surrounding area was flooded on several occasions, causing a great deal of damage to nearby houses.

After a petition of redress to Tynwald from local residents, a government scheme was completed in 2006 to protect the properties. As well as a wall alongside the river, a 'Flood Attenuation Lake' (somewhere to hold the flood water) was created in the field behind the houses.

◄ **Sulby Reservoir** was looking rather low during the summer of 2018, and for a brief period a hosepipe ban was in force throughout the Island. Will global warming mean this will happen every year?

► The hill farm of **Killabregga** had been abandoned by the 1940s, but a hundred years earlier, so records tell, there were fifteen people living in the two cottages on this tiny holding: Mr and Mrs Kinrade and their four sons and four daughters in one house, and Mr Kinrade's mother as well as his three bachelor brothers and a spinster sister in the other.

◀   This magnificent view of **Kerroogarroo Fort**, just north of St Jude's, gives a good idea of its extraordinary shape, which is not obvious from the ground.

Built during the 1640s by James, 7th Earl of Derby, the fort was intended to defend the north of the Island from any invading army.

Such an army did actually arrive during the English Civil War, but by the time they got to the Island this fort, along with all the others, had surrendered to the forces of William Christian (Illiam Dhone), who then surrendered the Island to the Parliamentary forces anchored in Ramsey Bay.

The fort has diamond-shaped bastions at each corner from where canon could fire down on attackers, and there would have been a strong, wooden paling fence running round the top to protect the soldiers inside.

Apart from a short altercation when the fort was captured (no shots were fired - it was just a shouting match), it never saw any real action and nowadays it is a peaceful place to visit on a summer's day when the view south to the hills presents a stunning backdrop.

▼   At the foot of Snaefell is this extraordinary sight - the spoil heaps from the **Snaefell Mine**. Trials were started in this area in the 1840s and eventually a shaft was dug to a depth of 1,026ft.

Sadly, it is now known as the site of the Island's worst mining disaster when, on the morning of 10th May 1897, miners, descending to start their shift, were overcome by deadly carbon monoxide gas. Twenty miners lost their lives. Above the spoil heaps can be seen the small, double-walled stone building where the explosives were kept and above that, one of the more extraordinary constructions on the Isle of Man. It is actually a long, narrow reservoir which curves round the side of the mountain for nearly half a mile. It is supported by a massive retaining wall, now covered in grass and ferns. The water captured here was used to drive a 50ft waterwheel that once powered the lifting gear in the mine.

In the 1950s a licence was issued to a company called Metalliferous Holdings Ltd who reworked the mines using more modern techniques to extract, any metal ores that had been left behind from the previous operation. Most of the buildings and the fine, grey deposits which now scar the landscape, date from this period.

► At one time, Manx prisoners were held in Castle Rushen, then they were held in a Victorian prison in Douglas, which long outstayed its welcome. Nowadays they have the most modern accommodation.

Jurby Prison was opened in 2008, after prolonged debates in Tynwald about where the new facility should be located. Some MHKs quite clearly didn't want it in their constituency. It is a great improvement on previous Manx prisons. All prisoners have their own cells equipped with their own toilet and washing facilities, and a wide variety of educational and vocational training is also available.

► Just south of the prison is a strange situation, a house desperately trying not to fall into the sea. Erosion is a continuing problem along the northern coasts and many houses have already fallen into the sea in the past two centuries. Here at **Killane**, the old mill (built in 1504 when it was a long way inland), is now protected by a wall of granite boulders, built to try and mitigate the effects of the sea.

Unfortunately, such structures often pass the problem along the coast and these defences have accelerated the erosion in front of his neighbour, who has had to place boulders at the bottom of his garden as well. The outline of the old mill pond is visible behind the mill.

◀ **Kirk Michael**, on the west coast of the Island, has one or two unique features about it.

For some reason, it is the only town or village on the Island which doesn't have any local authority housing. Apparently, in the years after the war, the Manx government contacted all the towns and villages asking them if they would like to accommodate local authority housing, and Kirk Michael was the only one to say 'no thanks'. However, there's something much more pressing to occupy the minds of the residents. How many of them know about it?

In a report presented to Tynwald in 2001 by engineering consultants Posford Duvivier, commissioned to take a detailed look at the rates of coastal erosion round the north of the Island, it was claimed that before the end of this century most of the land on the seaward side of the main road will have gone; fallen into the sea!

The stoic residents of the village seem to have taken it in their stride, and there certainly isn't an air of panic when you visit. In fact, in an act of total defiance, a new housing estate has been built but a stone's throw from the edge of the sand cliffs. Its local nickname is the King Canute Estate.

◀ **The Glen Wyllin Trout Farm** sells eggs to over 50 countries around the world, exporting millions every year.

▲ Where the sand cliffs dip down there has been some attempt to slow coastal erosion by the placing of granite boulders. More boulders have been placed a short distance further down the coast. Unfortunately, such isolated placements tend to exacerbate erosion immediately up the coast from where they are. In the case of the furthest boulders, you can see how the land in front of the trout farm is being eaten away. It's a pity that the two sections of boulders hadn't been joined together, thereby providing some protection for the land in between.

◀ A view looking down on the popular **Glen Wyllin** with the new estate of Broogh Wyllin in the distance (*top left*), a few yards from the eroding cliff edge. The planning application for this estate was turned down by the local commissioners and by the planning committee, but both were overruled and the government let the development go ahead. It was built for first time buyers, though some sarcastically say it is now for last time buyers.

PEEL &
THE WEST

▲ The northern end of **Peel Promenade** is part of one of the finest bays on the Island. With its sandy beach, views of the castle and endless ice cream, Peel is an increasingly popular destination for families and tourists, as well as those attending the many events that are staged here throughout the year.

▶ Perhaps one of the most romantic views on the Island, **Peel Castle** on St Michael's Isle (*opposite*) is steeped in history. The isle has been inhabited since prehistoric times and the visible remains date from the 10th century. Joined by a causeway since 1796, the isle is a popular place for walks, food and fishing.

◄ The quayside in **Peel** presents a pleasing array of buildings of all shapes and sizes, some of them dating back several centuries to when smuggling was the main income of the Manx.

In the foreground a coach has just arrived. Manx tourism is seeing a steady revival and a visit to Peel, with its narrow, winding streets, marina, castle and museums is one of the highlights, especially when you can buy freshly smoked kippers while you're here.

◄ Unlike Ramsey, Peel seized the opportunity to have a marina and it has made a dramatic difference to the area, almost as dramatic as the monstrous chimney of the power station. Built in 1994 it is still difficult to ignore it, especially as the power station is now only used occasionally as back-up, or to supply power to the UK when loads demand it.

▲ A dramatic view of **St German's Cathedral** within the walls of Peel Castle. It was started in the 13th century and its precinct wall would once have gone out as far as the two little gateposts which are now left, forlornly, in the middle of the grass. To the left of the cathedral are the remains of the Lord of Mann's apartments which date from the 15th century and were in use until the 18th century.

◀ **Peel Police Station** (*far left*) stands in its own grounds at the entrance to the Cathedral grounds (*left*) which are undergoing a major redevelopment. A series of seventeen conceptual gardens are being developed around the Cathedral, one of them, the Abbey Garden with its 13th century labyrinth, is clearly visible from above.

◀ Peel has seen a boom in house building in recent years, and there has been a parallel increase in population. The edges of the town are now dedicated to housing estates (*below, left*) and hopefully this increase will have a beneficial effect on the economy of the town.

▲ The tiny cove of **Niarbyl** (*above*) has appeared in a number of feature films, mostly because of its quaint thatched cottages.

▲ **Milner's Tower**, on the summit of Bradda Head overlooking Port Erin bay, was built to resemble an old key and as a tribute to William Milner, a safe maker and benefactor of the poor of Port Erin.

◄ **Niarbyl** gets its name from the Manx *Yn Arbyl*, which means 'a tail', and indeed, there is a tail of rocks which juts out into the sea, shining in the sunlight.

◄   Milner's Tower stands on
Bradda Head, which commands
views across Port Erin bay and on to
the south and the Calf of Man.
Apart from being a striking feature
when viewed from Port Erin itself,
the head is riddled with valuable ore,
and since as far back as the Bronze
Age intrepid miners have scaled its
cliffs and burrowed into its interior,
following the rich veins of copper
that led them ever deeper into the
rock.

▶   Next to the The **Cosy Nook Cafe** (top left, opposite) on the beach at Port Erin is the elegant tower of one of the leading lights which line up to help vessels coming into the bay avoid the submerged breakwater. The block of four hotels above the cafe have since been demolished. The Cherry Orchard Hotel (top right) closed in 2017, but the apartments, the swimming pool and the self-catering apartments still remain. The Upper Promenade (bottom left) leads on to the small community of Spaldrick (bottom right) to the left of which is a remarkable building once known as Collinson's cafe. It's Edwardian and once housed a cafe and a sprung dance floor and it had its own resident orchestra. It was a popular meeting place for internees in the Rushen Internment Camp during World War II.

▲   It is barely believable that men scrambled down this cliff at the **North Bradda Mines** to go deep inside the headland in search of copper ore, which can be seen staining the cliffs bright green just above the high tide.

Some of the mine levels went out beneath the sea, as well as high up into the head itself. One of the entrances can be seen next to the old engine house, which clings precariously to the cliff face. How did they get all the materials down here to build such a structure, and how did they get the mined ore away from the site? It would be far too treacherous to bring a boat in here.

Sadly, there are no photographs, no drawings and no first-hand accounts of how these workings operated, so we can only marvel at how things might have been.

◀ At the bottom of this photograph of **Port Erin** is a cove with the remains of a building and slipway. This was once the site of the original Marine Biological station set up by a Liverpool committee in 1892. Much of their work involved dredging excursions in the Irish Sea but, with the growing number of tourists and visiting naturalists, it was decided to relocate the station to the south-west corner of the bay, and only the foundations of the old station remain.

Above, there is a series of winding paths that provide popular walks, though they are precariously close to the edge of the cliffs.
To the right, across the road, is the cleared site of one of the last of the great seafront hotels that made Port Erin's bay so distinctive.

The Port Erin Royal, which stood behind the blue hoarding, was demolished in August 2017. It had been closed for nearly ten years.
In the distance is the Rowany Golf Club and beyond, the gap in the hills which is Fleshwick. Even a place as remote as that was exploited for the burgeoning tourist industry with a small cafe on the road down to the beach.

◀ **Port Erin** has really developed in three stages - the original fishing village along the shore, the Victorian and Edwardian hotels on the promenade above and now, behind, a sea of bungalows and housing estates.

Many of the original cottages survive, including the row built by philanthropist William Milner with their gardens across Shore Road. Up above, things are somewhat different. The long line of hotels which once graced the upper promenade have all gone, to be replaced with modern apartments, but, although the number of tourists coming to the Island has declined dramatically since the early 20th century, Port Erin beach seems to be more popular than ever.

On a summer's day during the school holidays the kayaks are out, youngsters are taking dinghy lessons, and sea bathing and sandcastle building are as popular as ever.

CASTLETOWN & THE EAST

▲   In the foreground is **Kitterland**, sitting in the middle of The Sound, the narrow channel between the Calf of Man and the main Island. Usually it's occupied by seals who bask on the rocks and provide endless entertainment for visitors gathered on the grass below the Sound cafe.

▶   On the **Calf of Man** itself are two magnificent Georgian lighthouses that celebrated their 200th anniversary in 2018. Built in 1818 by Robert Stevenson for the Northern Lighthouse Board, their synchronised beams lined up with the treacherous Chicken's Rock, a few hundred yards offshore. They were abandoned in 1874 when a tower light was built on the Chicken's and for a brief period in the 20th century another light was active on the Calf, but this, too, has now been abandoned.

◄ South Harbour is the preferred landing place on the **Calf of Man**, but is only accessible on either side of high tide. From here it is a relatively short walk to the early lighthouses, which is just about manageable on a day trip.

◄► The spectacular rock slides at the **chasms** give the impression that the coast here is just crumbling away. Actually, it is, but only in geological terms. It will be many thousands of years before it looks much different from this, although the exceptionally dry summer of 2018 has given the area an uncharacteristically brown look.

One bit of rock that stands out from the rest is the **Sugar Loaf** (*right*), home to huge numbers of sea birds including guillemots, razorbills and kittiwakes, a flock of which is wheeling above the sea.

◀▲ The drone was able to get close in to the **Sugar Loaf** (*above and left*) and on the many ledges the nesting guillemots are quite unconcerned by the flying camera. Although the drone makes a noise like a swarm of bees, this was as nothing compared to the racket the birds make, which can be heard a mile away at the top of the chasms.

After rearing their young and watching them fledge, the entire colony, on a single day, will leave the Sugar Loaf and may not touch land again for many months. An eerie silence descends on the cliffs with only the seagulls and choughs for company.

▶ The circular aircraft-tracking mech disk, to the east of Cregneash, looks like some alien ship has landed and the passengers have gone to the Creg y Shee cafe for afternoon tea. Let's hope they brought some Manx money with them.

◄ Nestled below the summit of Meayll Hill is the small village of **Cregneash**, which nowadays is regarded as a 'folk village'. Some families still live here but most of the buildings are given over to depicting life in a small farming community as it might have been in the 19th and early 20th centuries. Here you can see examples of plough horses, Loaghtan sheep, tourists and, if you're lucky, a Manx cat.

◄   A view looking over The Point in **Port St Mary**.

The large, white building is also known as The Point. Once a hotel it is now an apartment block, described as being in the Art Deco Modern Movement style.
A second floor, two-bedroom apartment could set you back up to £375,000, but the views are great.

In the distance is an isolated house, square and white. This was once a hotel called the Clifton, but it was bought by band leader Ronnie Aldrich and renamed the Strathallen Castle.

Ronnie was musical director of the Squadronaires, a band started by the RAF in 1939 to raise morale. Eventually they became regulars here on the Isle of Man and Ronnie and his wife settled in Port St Mary.

▶ Looking the other way you can see the inner and outer piers of **Port St Mary's harbour**.

The outer pier, the Alfred Pier, lost its small cast iron light in a wild south-westerly storm in 2009. It was decided not to replace it.
In the far distance is Bay ny Carrickey with Gansey Point in between.

► Looking down on Bay View Road in **Port St Mary** (*right*) you can see The Cat Walk, a footpath which snakes along just above the rocks and provides a different perspective of the village.

Next to St Mary's Church on Bay View Road is a longish grey building with seven chimney stacks (*opposite page*).

Now privately owned, this was built by the Northern Lighthouse Board as a shore station for lighthouse keepers working on the Chicken's Rock. Their families lived here and the emblem and motto of the Board is still visible above the door.

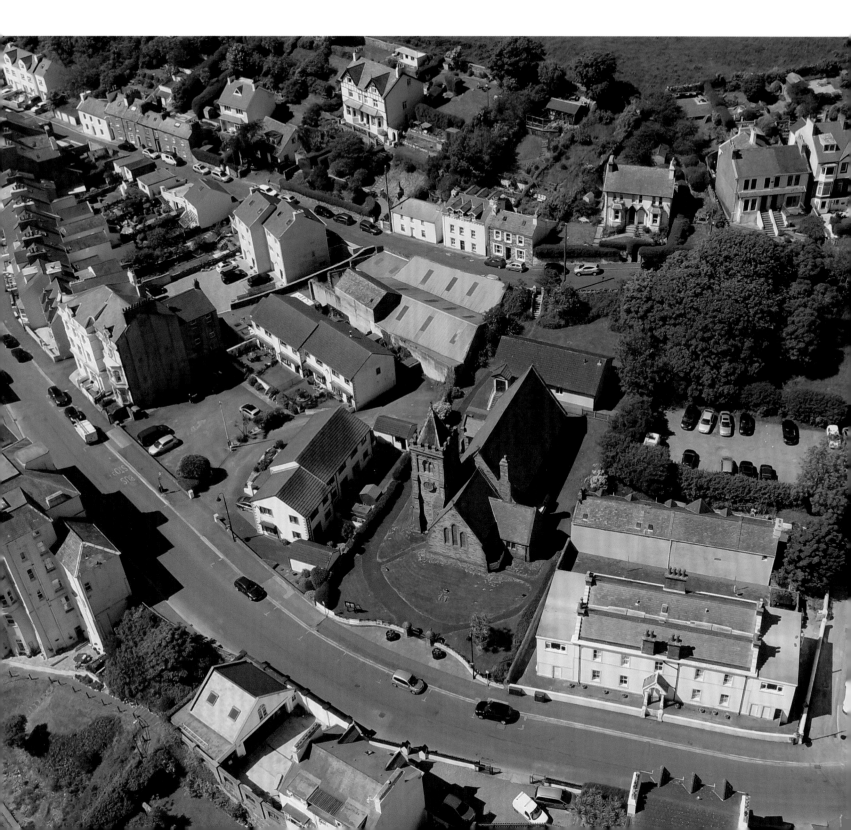

◄   When the tide goes out at **Port St Mary**, the inner harbour is dry and the boats sit on the mud.

Would a marina be a good idea? Well, this has actually been discussed for many years, but nothing has come of it so far.

However, in March 2018 the Manx government approved a scheme to spend £80m over a three-year period to improve Manx harbours, and part of that scheme might include a marina for the port.

◀ Chapel Bay is the main beach for **Port St Mary** and there's a fine terrace of Victorian houses sitting above, many of which were once boarding houses but most of which are now private houses divided into apartments.

At the end of the terrace is the greatest of them all, the Bay Queen Hotel of which many people have the fondest of memories. However, it has been empty and derelict for many years, and part of it had to be demolished.

A local developer has plans to create two separate blocks on the site, each containing 45 apartments, though as the remaining part of the hotel is on the register of protected buildings, taking it off the register is the first step before demolition.
It is not unknown for approval for this sort of action to be given on the Isle of Man.

▶ **Castletown**, the old capital of the Isle of Man.

The breakwater offers some protection from easterlies for the entrance to the harbour, but it's never been an easy port to enter and it is really the great medieval castle at its centre which has been the driving force in developing the town over the centuries.

For many decades the town was landlocked, and development on its edges was severly restricted due to landowners not wanting to sell, but in recent years there has been a tentative push into the surrounding countryside, and more is promised.

In the distance, peeping through the trees, is the mansion of Balladoole, once the home of the Stevenson family.

On the edge of the town can be seen the pink-rendered tower of the so-called Witches Mill. It once contained a museum of witchcraft, but at one time it was a genuine windmill and it must have looked very dramatic when it had its giant sails attached.

◀ Looking down onto **Castletown Harbour** there is an extraordinary array of historic buildings.

The tall grey building, covered in slates, is Bridge House, a huge Georgian town house built by the Quayle family. It has four stories with a cellar and attics, all built on a grand scale. A little slate-covered building to its side houses an old bank vault, built by one of the Quayles when he started his own bank at the beginning of the 19th century.

It is a masterpiece of eccentricity, the vault door being opened by a complex arrangement of ropes and pulleys. On its immediate right is the Nautical Museum with a old boathouse, and further towards the sea the houses all have protective walls to shelter them from the battering of the winter storms coming into the harbour.

◀   At the centre of **Castletown** sits Castle Rushen, a magnificent medieval structure built of local limestone and variously used for defence, a prison, a Lord's home, the Courts of Justice, and now, a tourist attraction.

There's no doubt that some of the nearby street alignments were established in medieval times and, as the old capital of the Island, there is a large number of fine Georgian houses nearby as well.

▶ Looking across the harbour (*right*), and hidden in the trees, is **Lorne House**, a Regency villa, once the home of the Lieutenant Governors of the Island and sitting on land of historic and great archaeological importance.

▶ The Governor was able to look directly across the harbour and see the walls of **Castle Rushen** (*opposite page*) surrounded by its battlements. The earliest part dates from the late 1100s when the central keep was started and towers were added to the west and south in the early 14th century. The main gate house is at the top of the picture with the apartments of the Earls of Derby extending down to the right.

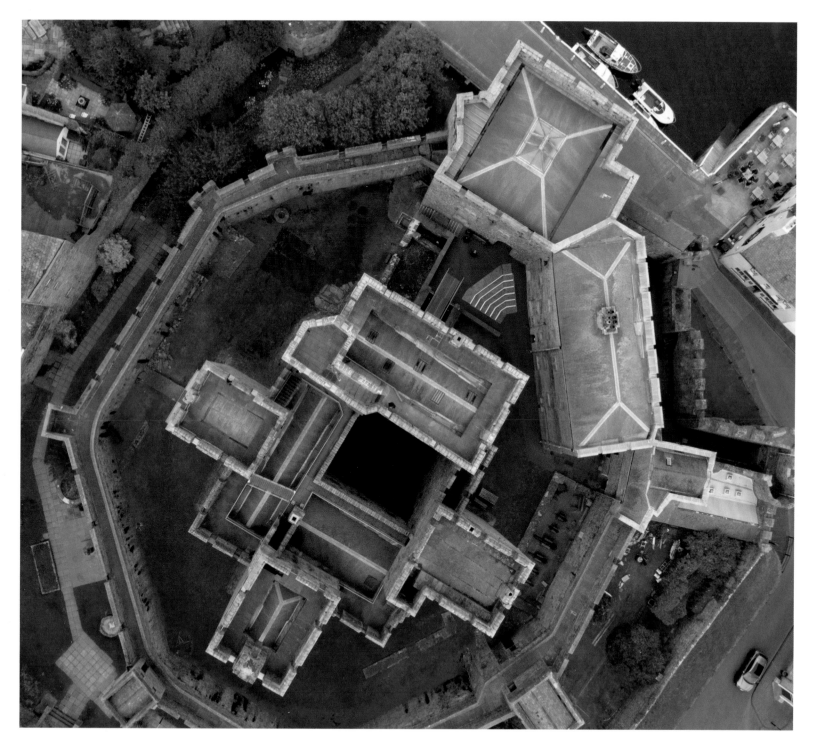

◄ The market square in **Castletown** has a single Doric column at its edge, placed there in 1837 to memorialise one of the Island's most popular Lieutenant Governors, Colonel Cornelius Smelt. However, the money ran out and the proposed statue of him to be placed on the top never materialised.

Beyond is the white, Gothic façade of St Mary's Church which was closed in 1977 as it had fallen into disrepair. Some years later it was sold off and turned into offices and it provides a fine backdrop to the Parade - the row of Georgian houses nearby.

◀   Looking east from Castletown you can see the estate of **Janet's Corner**, newly refurbished with a mixture of housing sporting red and grey roofs.

Quite who Janet was, no one's sure, but the area was first developed during World War II when the Fleet Air Arm set up a base there, entirely covered in Nissan Huts, to operate the nearby airfield, which eventually became Ronaldsway Airport.
On the edge of the airfield can be seen the grey mass of King William's College, a public school founded by Bishop Barrow in the 17th century, but not actually built until the 1830s.

▶ Out on the peninsular of Langness is a slate-built tower, popularly known as the **Herring Tower**.

It's been said that a lookout, stationed at its top. would spot the shoals of herring and indicate to the fishing vessels where they were. Sadly, an urban myth.

It would be impossible to shout to fishing boats from the top of the tower, even if you were foolish enough to climb up the narrow interior spiral staircase and could balance yourself there.

It is actually a marker tower, put there in the years before lighthouses were built to mark one piece of land from another, all of which can look very similar on grey, rainy days.

There's no doubt that the herring boats would have used it as a guide back into Derbyhaven bay, but it was never used to find their catch for them. The western side of the tower is gradually losing its render after being exposed to westerly gales for a couple of centuries.

The last tower to suffer from this was the old chimney at Beckwith's Mine. It collapsed in 2012.

▶ Looking out over the
Langness Peninsular (*right*) you
can see the walled enclosure and
buildings of Langness Lighthouse.

Built in 1880, it is now automated
and the cottages have been sold
into private ownership.
To the left can be seen six little
dots on the landscape. They are
circular brick gun emplacements
from the Second World War.

Stretching out to the right is
Dreswick Point, actually the
Island's most southerly tip.

▶ A dramatic aerial view of the
Derby Fort at the entrance to
Derbyhaven Bay (*opposite page*).
It was improved by the 7th Earl of
Derby in the 1640s but an earlier
version probably existed for at
least 100 years before.

The remains of interior buildings
can be seen and the seven canon
ports all point across the bay to
defend its entrance.

◀ **Ronaldsway Airport**
actually dates back to 1933 when
the Blackpool and West Coast Air
Services started, but there were no
facilities here and the nearby
Derbyhaven Hotel was used as a
gathering place for passengers.
During the war the area was
commandeered by the Fleet Air Arm
who established HMS *Urley* for
training purposes, and after the war
the airfield was developed as the Isle
of Man's main airport.

Nowadays there are more than
23,000 aircraft movements a year,
carrying in excess of 800,000
passengers.

▲ Finally, back at Douglas again, here is the splendid **Douglas Lighthouse**, built in 1892 and a marker for the hundreds of thousands of sea travellers who have come and gone through the port of Douglas over the past 120 years.